Live Better pilates

Live Better pilates

exercises and inspirations for well-being

Karen Smith

DUNCAN BAIRD PUBLISHERS

LONDON

Live Better: Pilates

Karen Smith

For Gordon Thomson – my first Pilates teacher.

First published in the United Kingdom
and Ireland in 2006 by
Duncan Baird Publishers Ltd
Sixth Floor
Castle House
75–76 Wells Street
London W1T 3QH

Conceived, created and designed by
Duncan Baird Publishers Ltd

Managing Designer: Manisha Patel
Designer: Justin Ford
Managing Editor: Grace Cheetham
Editor: Zoë Fargher
Picture Research: Julia Ruxton
Commissioned Photography: Matthew Ward

British Library Cataloguing-in-Publication Data:
A CIP record for this book is available from the
British Library.

ISBN: 978-1-84483-240-8

10 9 8 7 6 5 4 3 2

Typeset in Filosofia and Son Kern
Colour reproduction by Scanhouse, Malaysia
Printed by Imago, Malaysia

Publisher's note

contents

Introduction

I have been practising Pilates for nearly 25 years. As a ballet dancer during the 1970s and early 1980s I was aware of its existence, but there were few Pilates studios around and I was always too busy touring, rehearsing and performing to incorporate it into my lifestyle.

It was after a terrible car accident in which I broke my neck and was totally paralyzed for nearly three months, that I realized the tremendous benefits of this unique exercise method. When I left hospital my weight had dropped to around five stone, my muscles were atrophied and my confidence was at an all-time low.

I began attending Pilates sessions twice a week in a beautifully equipped studio. Lying on the reformer machine on my back, with my head, neck and spine fully supported, I was able to work my limbs and abdominal muscles, gradually toning and strengthening them. The results were amazing. Within about three months my body was transformed from a weak and feeble, almost skeletal specimen to a normal-looking, stronger body.

The beauty of Pilates is that everyone can benefit from it, no matter what your age. My youngest client at the moment is nine and my eldest in her eighties. And nowadays Pilates is more accessible owing to the increase in the number of studios and matwork classes.

It is the matwork that this book illustrates. It gives you a basic foundation to make Pilates a part of your life. Starting with a little background information, Chapter 1 outlines the main principles of Pilates, how to breathe correctly in order to carry out the exercises properly, and the importance of core stability, without which Pilates exercises would be totally impractical.

After a brief warm-up in Chapter 2, I have explained a number of exercises in chapters 3, 4 and 5 that I teach on a daily basis, focusing on the abdominals, the back, neck and shoulders, and the arms, legs and feet. Finally in Chapter 6 there are some Pilates exercise sequences, suggested exercises for sports people, a short section on relaxation, and help on finding a teacher.

I hope that Pilates will help you to live better and feel stronger as much as it helped me.

Chapter One

origins and basics

Pilates has been around for more than 80 years. Originally it was taught in studios using equipment designed by Joseph Pilates himself. These machines work by using springs, pulleys and weights to provide resistance for the muscles to work against. Unlike in a gym, the client is always supervised. However, because these studios were fairly rare, a program of "floor exercises", nowadays known as matwork, was developed which has gradually made Pilates more accessible and affordable over recent years.

Pilates exercise is extremely precise, so it is important that you pay particular attention to your body alignment when practising. In this chapter you will learn the key principles of Pilates, all of which play a role in the execution of the exercises. Once you start practising, you will understand the importance of Pilates as a means of rebalancing certain areas of the body and strengthening weak areas.

The most important aspect of Pilates exercise is working from a strong centre. This is outlined in the sections on core stability and pelvic floor. The breathing is usually the hardest part to master but it will become second nature with time. Make sure you read this chapter before starting the exercises – it will help you to understand the basic fundamentals and achieve the most out of your practice.

WHY PRACTISE PILATES?

Pilates is a form of exercise that co-ordinates the working of muscles with the breathing. It tones and strengthens the whole body, and improves posture using a carefully developed method perfected over a period of more than seventy years' experience.

Its creator, Joseph Hubertus Pilates, was born in Germany in 1880. As a child he suffered from asthma, rickets, and rheumatic fever. He strove to overcome his fragility and physical ailments and achieve a strong, healthy body by integrating elements of martial arts, yoga and meditation with aerobic sports and strength conditioning. He discovered that by using his mind and body together he could strengthen the deep postural muscles to correct muscle imbalances, improve posture, protect his lower back and condition his entire body. Eventually he became a keen sportsman, a gymnast, a skier, a diver, a boxer and a circus performer.

In 1912 Pilates travelled to England, where he was interned when the First World War broke out. Helping out in the camp infirmary, he further developed his innovative ideas about health and physical fitness. He experimented with springs, attached to hospital beds, that enabled patients to tone and stretch their muscles through resistance exercises. Eventually he designed a machine called the Universal Reformer which is still used today, together with other machines he created.

After the war Pilates returned to Germany and worked on movement techniques, notably with Rudolf von Laban, the creator of a dance notation form still used today. In 1926 he left Germany and set up a studio in New York which attracted dancers, actors, gymnasts and athletes. He died in 1967 at the age of 87.

His training regime, which became known simply as Pilates, has now been taught for more than eighty years, yet it is only during the last few years that it has become a mainstream form of exercise. In addition, many medical professionals, osteopaths and physiotherapists have realized the efficacy of the Pilates system in preventing and rehabilitating injuries, and many now include Pilates as a complementary addition to their treatment.

One of the reasons Pilates is so successful is because it focuses on the body as a whole, and on working with people as individuals. The exercises can vary from day to day, week to week just as someone's body can change. Many other fitness regimes are concerned with one or two specific areas of the body such as "bums and tums" or "hips and thighs". With Pilates it is less about "what" you do, and more about "how" you do it. Rather than doing fifty "crunches" at the gym, paying no attention to alignment and core stability, students in a Pilates class will practise ten correctly positioned, slower "curl-ups".

As a result of the Pilates method there are far fewer injuries overall, and in fact teachers are very often faced with clients who have injured themselves at gyms through over-straining or poor body awareness.

Pilates practitioners can achieve the flat stomachs, lean legs and toned buttocks but with far more lasting results. In short ten good reasons to practise Pilates are:

- Restores flexibility and joint mobility
- Improves balance, co-ordination and alignment
- Eliminates bad postural habits

- Tones slack muscles
- Improves body awareness
- Reduces tension
- Prevents injuries
- Allows the body to function more efficiently
- Alleviates back pain

Anyone who wishes to improve their total fitness, posture and appearance can practise Pilates exercises. Because the exercises are so precise and they strengthen and tone the body with minimal risk of injury, Pilates can also be useful to:

- Chronic back pain sufferers
- R.S.I. (repetitive strain injury) sufferers
- First-time exercisers
- The elderly
- Those wishing to help prevent or alleviate osteoporosis
- Sports people, athletes, dancers, musicians and all performers to whom good posture is vital
- Anyone with a sedentary lifestyle
- Basically anyone irrespective of age and fitness level!

KEY PRINCIPLES
OF THE PILATES METHOD

Every Pilates exercise is centred around the eight basic
principles of Pilates, as follows:

- **Alignment** Correct alignment is so important for every
  movement in every exercise. Try to visualize your body
  like building blocks – the head is over the ribcage over
  the pelvis, which is over each leg, which is over each foot.
- **Breathing** Lateral or thoracic breathing is the key to
  Pilates. This entails learning to breathe into the ribcage
  rather than the abdomen. Breathing is integral to the
  timing of the exercises, and, when mastered, this form
  of breathing will actually increase lung capacity.
- **Centring** This forms a crucial starting point for each
  exercise. You are aiming to establish a stable central
  core around which movement takes place. The main
  reason for this is to create a muscular "corset" to keep
  the pelvis and spine stable (see page 20), particularly
  important in the rehabilitation of back problems.

- **Concentration** Pilates is often quoted as the "thinking person's exercise". Ideally the movements should originate in the mind. This way you can really feel a movement rather than just execute the exercise.

- **Co-ordination** The principle of co-ordination works alongside concentration. The mind should work ahead of the body so that you always know in advance what the movement will be and how to co-ordinate the breathing.

- **Flowing movements** With the body correctly aligned, energy flows freely and "blocks" are eliminated. The aim is to move through each sequence of an exercise with optimal mechanical efficiency, maintaining the flow and rhythm of its movement.

- **Relaxation** When practising Pilates it is important not to over-strain the body, but use just the right amount of tension to achieve the movement. The secret lies in knowing how to work the relevant area, and perform the exercise without tensing the surrounding muscles.

- **Stamina** While Pilates is non-aerobic generally, your stamina and the endurance of your postural muscles will improve with time, as will your mental stamina.

Learn to listen to the voice within yourself. Your body
and mind will become clear and you will realize the
unity of all things.

DOGEN

(1200–1253BCE)

Take care of your body with steadfast fidelity. The soul
must see through these eyes alone, and if they are dim,
the whole world is clouded.

JOHANN WOLFGANG VON GOETHE

(1749–1832)

FINDING YOUR BALANCE

1 Stand in front of a mirror with your feet slightly apart. Look in the mirror and check whether your head tilts to one side, if so correct it. Now imagine you had a balloon attached to a string on the top of your head, giving it a feeling of weightlessness. Allow the neck to release and lengthen, and be careful that the chin does not jut out or drop down toward the floor.

2 Now look at your shoulders. Is one higher than the other? Gently correct them so that they are level. Allow the arms to hang heavily from the shoulder joints with no tension in the wrists or hands. Don't be tempted to pull the shoulders too far back as this can create tension in the upper back. Soften the upper chest and the breastbone to enable the upper back to slightly widen. Draw your abdominals in toward your lower back. This is often referred to as "navel to spine" in Pilates and is the starting point for every exercise.

3 Lengthen the tailbone toward the floor as if you had a small weight attached to it. Be careful not to "tuck" it

under the hips. Check your hips, and correct them if one hip looks higher than the other. Release the front of the hips so that they are not gripping, and relax the front of the thighs. Feel that your legs are lengthening, but avoid locking into the backs of the knees. Check that the knees are in line with the front of the hips and ankles and are not swinging outward or twisting inward.

4 Take your body weight forward on the balls of the feet and toes and then transfer it back on to your heels. Now find a point in the middle to settle your balance. Keep the weight carefully and evenly distributed between your heels, big toes and little toes. These are your three secure points of balance, like a tripod.

5 Now that you have found your balance and correct standing posture check once again: your head should rest comfortably on your neck. From here there is a plumb line down to the pubic bone. The shoulders are level and are over the hips. The hips are level and lie over the knees, which are aligned over the ankles. Close your eyes for a few moments to really feel the position, so that you can absorb it into your physical memory.

WHAT IS CORE STABILITY?

The aim of Pilates is to create a strong and stable centre to support and protect the lower back while the limbs move freely. This is the "girdle of strength" that Joseph Pilates maintained as being one of the most important principles of his exercise method, and which is also often referred to as core stability.

The core of the body is the part between the pelvis and the ribcage, and this relies on certain muscles to hold it strong. Four large muscles wrap around the abdomen, which support the internal organs and hold them in place. These are the rectus abdominis, transverse abdominis and the internal and external obliques. Like a corset the tighter and stronger they are, the more support they will provide. Obviously you don't want to walk around all day long straining to keep these muscles engaged, otherwise they will become tired. Ideally you want to learn how to turn the muscles on and off so that you can use them to stabilize the body when you need them to and allow them to rest when you don't.

The simple act of coughing will cause these muscles to tighten and the not-so-simple act of natural childbirth also relies on them to a certain degree. You should begin each Pilates exercise by drawing your abdominal centre inward, a movement often referred to as "navel to spine". You also need to engage the pelvic floor and the "lats" (latissimus dorsi). Although this might seem rather a lot to have to think about and co-ordinate, after a while it will become second nature.

Once you get the feel for using your core muscles you will be able to incorporate them into everyday activities such as lifting and gardening. This will protect you from injury, particularly to your back, and in the long run will give you a flatter stomach and a stronger back.

Here is an easy visualization that will help you to achieve "navel to spine" before you begin exercising. Imagine that there is a piece of string attached to your navel, running through your body and emerging from your spine at the back. As you adopt "navel to spine" it is as if someone is pulling the string to draw your navel closer to your backbone.

THE PELVIC FLOOR

The pelvic floor is a thin membrane consisting of layers of muscle and connective tissue. It is suspended across the pelvic girdle in both men and women.

The pelvic floor has two vital functions: it acts as a support for the organs of the abdomen – the intestines, the rectum, the bladder, and the womb in women; and it contains a passage for the urethra, the sex organs, the rectum, and for a baby during birth. Without the support of the pelvic floor muscles the abdominal organs would fall or "prolapse" through the opening in the pelvic girdle. This is why it is so important to maintain strength and elasticity in this area.

In Pilates you need to use the pelvic floor in connection with your breathing and your centring. Weak pelvic floor muscles affect the lower back as the pelvis has less support. This can change the position and alignment of the lower spine and eventually cause back pain.

If you are not used to exercising your pelvic floor muscles it can be hard to locate them at first, especially if they have lost tone. Some women become aware of their pelvic floor muscles only through pregnancy! Unlike the other muscles of the body you can't "see" the pelvic floor muscles so visualization will help you to feel them a little more easily. Here is a simple exercise to get you started.

1 Sit on an upright chair with your back straight. Check that you have your weight evenly distributed on both buttocks by sitting high on your "sit" bones. Position the feet slightly apart.

2 Breathe in without lifting the shoulders and feel the spine lengthen up.

3 As you breathe out slowly lift the muscles between your pubic bone and the tailbone. Imagine you were trying to stop the flow of urine.

4 Breathe in and completely relax again.

5 As you breathe out try to engage your core abdominal muscles at the same time as your pelvic floor.

Once you develop a feel for your pelvic floor muscles you can increase the number of lifts and incorporate them into your everyday activities such as when you are travelling, sitting at a desk or standing in a queue.

WHAT IS SHOULDER STABILITY?

Like core stability, where you stabilize the lumbar and abdominal area while moving your limbs, shoulder stabilization means stabilizing the shoulder girdle while moving your arms. Stable shoulder-girdle muscles give a true range of movement to the shoulder joint.

Most of us hold a lot of tension in the neck without being aware of it. Activities such as sitting hunched over a desk all day, driving, carrying shopping or lifting babies can cause the muscles of the neck and upper shoulders to overwork, while the muscles of the upper and mid-back become over-stretched and therefore weaker. The result is very often headaches and neck tension, and the shoulders may be pulled forward giving a "round-shouldered" appearance.

If you stand in front of a mirror and let your arms hang down by your sides, notice which way your palms are facing. If they tend to face backward this indicates that your chest and front-of-shoulder muscles are tight causing your arms to rotate inward. This can have a restrictive affect on your breathing. Ideally the palms should face in toward the body.

Pilates exercise focuses on the way you use the muscles of the upper body and strengthens the stabilizing muscles of the shoulder blades such as the mid- and lower trapezius, and the latissimus dorsi, or "lats" – the muscles behind the shoulder blades, which ideally should be the source of all arm and shoulder movement. The "lats" are the uppermost section of the Pilates "girdle of strength". Many people use the shoulders when they move their arms instead of the lats.

It will take a while to re-educate the body, so at first you just need to get used to releasing tension in your neck and shoulders. Gradually your chest muscles will soften and open out and instead of your shoulders creeping up toward your ears they will release down into your upper back, making your neck appear longer and your general posture look better. Once you locate and strengthen your lats, and strengthen your abdominal muscles, you will be surprised at how much tension will release in your neck, shoulders and lower back.

PILATES BREATHING

Joseph Pilates devised a particular way of breathing with his exercises, known as thoracic or lateral breathing. Yoga and many relaxation techniques instruct you to breathe deep into the abdomen, but in Pilates this is impossible as it conflicts with the principle of keeping our abdominal muscles engaged (see pages 20–21).

When breathing in most people lift their shoulders and their upper chest. The breath is usually too shallow causing the rib-cage to stiffen. Another common occurence when breathing in is to allow the abdominal muscles to relax and balloon outward.

Making the most of your lung capacity by breathing deeply helps to get the blood pumping around the body more efficiently, oxygenating the whole system. This improves general health by nourishing the tissues, nerves and organs. Deep breathing calms the nerves and regenerates vital energy. Here are a few simple guidelines to help you practise. Make sure you breathe in through the nose and out through the mouth.

Inhalation

1 As you breathe in try not to lift the shoulders or the breastbone. Breathe in to your mid-back. Imagine your lungs like bellows inflating as you inhale.

2 The ribcage should expand laterally (sideways). If you are wearing a bra, imagine the strap expanding.

3 Place the hands just under the breastbone so that your middle fingers are touching each other. As you inhale the fingers should part slightly. Do not force the "in" breath otherwise you may feel dizzy or light-headed.

Exhalation

1 As you breathe out the shoulders and breastbone remain relaxed. If you are lying down, relax into the floor. Imagine the lungs like bellows deflating.

2 Feel the ribs closing back together, the bra strap slightly loosening and the breastbone softening. Release any tension between the shoulder blades.

3 With the hands still under the breastbone the middle fingers should now come back together as you exhale. Allow the "out" breath to be full and relaxed.

PRACTICALITIES OF PILATES

All you need to practise Pilates is a small space, a little time and the inclination. Remember Pilates needs you to focus your mind on your body, so turn off your phone and sort out anything that may distract you. Here are a few guidelines to help you get started at home:

- Practise in a warm, ventilated room away from draughts.
- Leave at least an hour after a meal before exercising.
- Wear comfortable clothing that does not restrict your movements.
- Wear cotton socks or work in bare feet, but be careful that your feet do not slip.
- Play some relaxing background music, rather than anything upbeat or distracting.
- Use a towel or exercise mat to cushion your spine when lying down.
- Use a small cushion or book to rest your head on if you feel discomfort at the back of your neck when lying on your back, and a cushion or rolled-up towel to rest your head on when lying on your front.

- If your hair is long, tie it back off your face either at the nape of your neck or high up on top so that it is not uncomfortable when lying on your back.
- You may like to use a stretch band to provide resistance in some of the exercises.
- Eventually you may reach the stage where you wish to use some light weights for some of the arm and leg exercises.
- Focus on maintaining a strong "core" or "girdle of strength" while exercising.
- Relax into your breathing, inhaling through your nose and exhaling through your mouth.
- Do not do too many repetitions to start with. Start with the minimum guidelines and gradually increase.
- Relax a little between exercises to release any neck, shoulder or back tension.
- Do not exercise if you are feeling unwell and be extra careful if you have taken any painkillers, as they may mask warning pains in your muscles or joints.
- Consult your medical practitioner before you start Pilates exercises, especially if you are pregnant or undergoing any medical treatments.

We must learn not to disassociate the airy flower
from the earthy root, for the flower that is cut off from
its root fades, and its seeds are barren, whereas the
root, secure in mother earth, can produce flower after
flower and bring their fruit to maturity.

KABBALISTIC WISDOM

Stability is not immobility.

KLEMENS, PRINCE VON METTERNICH

(1773-1859)

warming-up

Warming-up means raising your body temperature. When you are warm your body is more flexible. This is because the connective tissues, the muscles, tendons and ligaments, are more pliable when they are warm.

Warming-up for Pilates is different to warming-up for sports or vigorous exercise. Because Pilates exercises are so precise, you need to locate, isolate and develop all the key areas you will be using so that you move correctly and exercise efficiently.

Before practising any of the exercises in this book, it is important to understand the terms "neutral spine" and "neutral pelvis". Your spine naturally has four curves, which enable the back to absorb shocks.

Certain repeated movements put stress on the spinal disks, ligaments and muscles. Your pelvis connects to the spine and is balanced on the hip joints. Tilting it one way or another will pull on the lower back and place stress on the spinal tissues. Maintaining a neutral position keeps the spinal tissues at their normal length and relieves pressure from the disks.

In the following pages I have given you simple guidelines to help you find the relaxation and neutral positions. I have also suggested four easy exercises to gently mobilize the neck, shoulders, spine and feet. The ball exercise is optional but will add a little gentle cardio exercise to your warm-up if you practise it.

FINDING NEUTRAL PELVIS AND NEUTRAL SPINE

The starting position for finding neutral pelvis and neutral spine is the "relaxation position". This position allows the spine to lengthen naturally and the lower back to release. Your thighs should also release and the front of the hips will open. Many of the Pilates exercises in this book start with you lying in this position, and it is also advisable to return to the relaxation position after your basic warm-up exercises.

1 Lie on your back with your knees bent, feet hip-width apart. Rest your head on a small pillow or book if needed.

2 Allow the spine to feel heavy without pushing it in to the floor. The feet should be placed securely and feel "grounded", as if they are in wet cement.

Once you are comfortable in the relaxation position, you can try finding your natural neutral pelvis and spine using this simple exercise. You can practise this either standing or sitting. Whichever way you choose make it your main Pilates task before you start your exercises.

1   Imagine you have a clock on your abdomen. Your navel is
    12 o'clock; your pubic bone six o'clock and your hip
    bones are three and nine o'clock.

2   Tilt your pelvis back toward 12 o'clock. Your pelvis will
    "tuck under", your waist will be pushed into the floor
    and the front of the hips will have tightened. Also notice
    that your tailbone will have lifted up and you will have
    lost the natural lumbar curve of the spine.

3   Now tilt the pelvis gently down toward six o'clock. Your
    lower back will have arched, your stomach will probably
    stick out and your ribs will have flared upward. Either of
    these positions can create back strain if they are part of
    your habitual posture.

4   Now aim for a neutral position between six and 12
    o'clock, the pelvis neither tucked nor arched, and the
    tailbone lengthened and relaxed on the floor. When you
    are correctly aligned, there will be a small, natural arch
    in your lower back; you should be able to place your fin-
    gers under your waist to make sure that your spine is not
    pushing in to the floor. Be very careful when engaging
    your lower abdominals not to tuck or tilt the pelvis.

WARM-UP SEQUENCES

Neck and shoulder release Stand on the centre of a stretch band with your feet hip-width apart, holding the ends of the band with your palms facing the hips. Relax the shoulders and draw in your abdominals. Nod the head forward, lift it up and turn it right and then left. Repeat four times. Gently circle the shoulders forward, up, back and down. Repeat five times in each direction. Using a stretch band will give you a little resistance.

Spine roll-down Stand with your spine in neutral position. Bend the knees so that they are in line with your ankles. Breathe in without raising the shoulders and breathe out allowing the head to gently nod forward. Keeping your navel to spine continue to roll the spine down in a wheel-like movement vertebra by vertebra. Your head and arms should hang heavy, but your abdominals and ribs are still lifted. Breathe in and breathe out to start rolling the spine back up, being careful to keep sliding the shoulders down into the back as you roll up the spine segmentally.

Foot rises Stand with the feet hip-width apart. Rise up on to your toes keeping your abdominals pulled in. As you lower bend one knee, then rise up again; bend the other knee as you lower again. If you feel you are losing your balance, practise this exercise holding on to a chair or windowsill. About twenty of these will soon have your feet, ankles and calves warmed up.

Bouncing on a ball If you have an exercise ball this is a gentle and safe way to exercise the heart and lungs. Simply sit on the ball with your back straight and stomach strong. Gently bounce up and down keeping your arms relaxed. When you feel more confident, gradually lift your arms in front of your chest.

The loftier the building, the deeper must the
foundation be laid.

THOMAS À KEMPIS

(1379-1471)

It is the mind itself which builds the body.

FREDERICK SCHILLER

(1759-1805)

the abdominals

According to Pilates theory all body movement should originate from a strong centre. I referred to this as the "girdle of strength" in Chapter 1. Strengthening your abdominals won't just give you an esthetic advantage (a flatter stomach), it will also free the small of the back and loosen the lumbar region.

If your abdominals are weak, you need to take care not to place strain on the other muscles in the back, shoulders or legs. Weak abdominals can have a profound effect on the lower back. They become more slack, which allows the pelvis to tip down, causing a pronounced hollow in the lower back. As the tummy gets bigger, more weight is carried in front of the line of gravity and the lower back arches to compensate. This explains why pregnant women, who of course are carrying extra weight, often suffer from backache.

Once you are familiar with using your abdominals, you should aim to use the pelvic floor in conjunction with them. This will enable you to work the deeper underlying muscles more efficiently. Imagine you are wearing a corset that has been laced up around your middle. This is the support that you should always feel around your abdomen, regardless of which area of your body you are exercising. The following exercises will target your abdominal muscles. Make sure you maintain your neutral pelvis throughout.

ABDOMINAL CURL-UPS

1 Start in the relaxation position, with the hands gently supporting the back of the head and the elbows slightly lifted so you can see them within your peripheral vision. Breathe in without the shoulders lifting.

2 As you breathe out draw the abdominals in and slowly curl the head, neck, and top of the shoulders up so that your eye line is between your knees. Make sure you have not come out of your neutral pelvic position. The tailbone should be heavy and the front of the hips relaxed. Breathe in as you slowly curl back down. Repeat the exercise four to seven times. Practise your curl-ups slowly with control, not as fast sit-ups. Your hands should form a good head support, but never pull the head forward; the"pull" should be from your abdominal muscles and pelvic floor. If you feel a strain on your neck, support the head with a towel.

This exercise strengthens the abdominals and gently stretches the upper spine.

1

2

OBLIQUE CURL-UPS

1 Start in the relaxation position, again with the hands supporting the back of the head. Breathe in.

2 As you breathe out draw the navel to spine and curl up, taking your left shoulder or armpit toward the outside of your right knee. The left shoulder should remain open, and both shoulders slide down into your back. Keep your left hip firmly in position so that the pelvis does not tip to your right. Breathe in to slowly curl down. Breathe out and repeat to the other side. The knees should remain hip-width apart even though you are pulling across the body diagonally. If you are finding this difficult, place a cushion or ball between your knees. Breathe in to curl down. Repeat four to six times.

This exercise works the internal and external oblique muscles, which are like lattice work criss-crossing the abdomen, and are active when twisting and bending your trunk sideways. Working these muscles will improve your "girdle of strength" and tone the sides of your body.

1

2

SIDE HIP ROLLS

1 Start in the relaxation position with your feet and knees together. Your arms are resting on the floor by your sides. Your palms are facing downward, and your shoulders are sliding down into your back. Allow your spine to feel heavy and relaxed so that the ribs do not dome upwards. Breathe in.

2 Breathe out as you slowly roll your knees and hips to the right, gently turning your head to the left. Watch that you have not arched the back nor allowed the abdominals to pop out. The left shoulder should remain on the floor. Breathe in while you maintain this position. Breathe out using your abdominals and left external obliques to bring the knees and the hips back to the starting position. Breathe in and repeat on the left. Only roll as far as you are able to maintain core stability, and don't allow your legs to pull you out of position.

This exercise works the abdominal and oblique muscles and is a gentle rotation for the spine.

1

2

THE HUNDRED

1   Start in the relaxation position and carefully bend your right and then your left knee in toward your chest. Rest your head on a pillow if needed, and extend your arms alongside your body, palms down. The shoulders are down so that your "lats" are engaged. If you prefer you can rest your legs on an exercise ball or a chair.

2   Breathe in for five counts and breathe out for five counts. At the same time move your arms up and down in a pumping action, co-ordinating them with your counts. Do not let the arms touch the floor; they should stay level with your hips. As you inhale think of your lateral thoracic breathing, opening out the rib-cage without the abdominals popping up. As you exhale try to scoop your abdominals more. Isolate your arms from the shoulders. The shoulder girdle remains stable as the arms are pumping the air. Start off with four sets of ten breaths and gradually build up to ten sets, completing your full hundred. Eventually you will become strong enough to attempt the exercise with the head lifted.

1

2

The hundred stimulates circulation, co-ordinates breathing and movement and improves stamina. It also works the abdominals and strengthens the neck when the head is lifted.

CURL-DOWNS

1 Start sitting up with the knees bent and a stretch band or scarf around your feet. Your back should be straight and the pelvis balancing on your "sit" bones. Breathe in and, exhaling, curl back on to your tail bone, tilting the pelvis toward your feet. A band or scarf will give you support and resistance. Don't let the chin pull down too far.

2 Keep drawing the abdominals in and sliding the shoulders down so that the upper back does not hunch. Breathe in while holding your curl-down position and then breathe out to scoop up the abdominals and curl forward on to your "sit" bones, again lengthening up through the spine to straighten the back. Repeat four to seven times, aiming to go a little lower with each one to challenge your abdominals. Eventually you will be able to practise without the band or scarf.

This exercise strengthens the deep abdominals and increases the flexibility of the lower spine. It also works your "lats" if you keep the shoulders down toward the back of the ribcage.

1

2

THE STAR

1 Start this exercise lying prone on your stomach, with your arms extended outward above your head, which is resting on the floor or a small pillow. Your legs should be a little wider than hip-width apart and stretched out. If you suffer from lower back problems, place a pillow or flat cushion under your abdomen. Breathe in. Imagine you have a marble under your navel, and try to draw your navel away from it during this exercise.

2 Breathe out as you lift your right arm and left leg no more than 10cm (4in) off the floor. The aim is to do this without lifting the right shoulder and left hip, keeping the shoulder and pelvic girdle completely stable. Breathe in to lower the arm and leg. Breathe out to repeat with your left arm and right leg, remembering to draw the abdominals upward toward the lower spine without moving the pelvis. Keep your pubic bone and hip bones heavy to help you stabilize the pelvis. Repeat four times.

3 When you are stronger practise this exercise with your head raised about 5cm (2in) off the floor.

1

2

3

The aim of this exercise is to work and strengthen the back,
buttock and abdominal muscles.

Flow with whatever is happening and let
your mind be free.
Stay centred by accepting whatever you are doing.
This is the ultimate.

CHUANG TZU

(c.369BCE–286BCE)

Do not dwell in the past, do not dream of the future,
concentrate the mind on the present moment.

BUDDHA

(c.563–c483BCE)

the back, neck and shoulders

We are all taller first thing in the morning because the weight is taken off the spine while we sleep, and the disks widen a little. Once we stand up and move about gravity takes over, causing the spine to shorten during the day. A major cause of backache is a tight inflexible spine, which may result in certain parts of it becoming locked, and places stress on other areas of the body.

The neck and shoulders are also a main area for tension and stiffness. The weight of an average human head is between 3 and 4.5 kilos (7–10 lb), supported by the structure and muscles of the neck and shoulders. People who have stressful, sedentary jobs will suffer from tension in this area, and at times of mental and emotional stress our shoulders tighten, pulling on our upper-back muscles. This limits the expansion in our chest and ribs, restricting our breathing. In Pilates we aim to relax and lengthen the neck and release the shoulders by sliding them down. By releasing the neck you will have more freedom of movement for the head, and once your shoulders are stabilized you will create a wider range of movement for the arms. This chapter takes you through some exercises to both strengthen and release tension in the back, neck and shoulders.

SPINE CURLS

1   Begin in the relaxation position with the feet a little
closer to your buttocks than normal. Breathe in. Breathe
out to tilt your pelvis so that your pubic bone and tailbone curl away from the floor. Keeping the abdominals
strong, breathe in as you hold this position. Breathe out
to curl the lower part of the spine back to the floor, so
the tailbone is the last part to touch down. Breathe in.

2   Breathe out, and this time curl the spine a little higher
up – not too high, just to the level of the shoulder blades.
Keep your pelvis level and the buttock muscles strong,
not clenched, but tightened to help support the pelvis in
the elevated position. It is the combination of abdominal and buttock strength that should be helping you to
curl up and curl down. Do not allow your back muscles to
strain. Aim to articulate the spine vertebra by vertebra
in a wheel-like movement. Repeat five to seven times,
keeping the head, neck and shoulders relaxed. Once you
are used to the exercise, reach your arms behind the
head for an extra stretch.

1

2

The main aim of this exercise is to mobilize the spine and work the buttock muscles.

SPINE EXTENSION

1   This exercise works the spine in the opposite way to the previous exercise. Lie in the prone position (on your front) feet parallel, hip-width apart. Place your bent arms so that your hands are slightly forward of your head. Draw your abdominals away from the floor, and keep the lower back lengthened. Breathe in.

2   As you breathe out slide your shoulder blades down toward the back of your ribcage and lift your head away from the floor without bending your neck. Imagine you are looking into a mirror which is lying on the floor under your face. Breathe in to rest the head back on the floor. Breathe out and raise the upper body a little more this time still keeping your focus on the floor. Feel broad across your chest and shoulders. Breathe in to lower. Repeat five to seven times.

In this exercise you are aiming to strengthen the main muscle that extends down the spine (the erector spinae), the lats, and the other shoulder-stabilizing muscles.

THE DART

1   Place a small cushion or folded towel under your fore-head. Your arms are lengthened down at your sides and the palms are up. Your legs are together and buttocks relaxed. Breathe in.

2   Breathe out to open out your shoulder blades, sliding them down into your back as you lift the forehead 2.5 cm (1 in) off the floor. At the same time turn your palms in to face the sides of your thighs and lengthen the fingers down toward the sides of your knees. Be careful not to pinch the shoulders together. The top of your head is lengthening forward and the tip of the tailbone is lengthening in the opposite direction. Breathe in. Breathe out to lower the head relaxing the arms and shoulders. Repeat five to seven times. When you feel ready, try to incorporate an inner-thigh squeeze. Simply keep the feet on the floor and squeeze the tops of the inner thighs together without moving the pelvis. Remember the abdominals should be scooping away from gravity and the neck remains long.

1

2

The aim of this exercise is to strengthen the back extensor muscles, stabilize the trunk, and work the shoulder muscles.

CAT STRETCH AND REST POSITION

1 It is advisable to practise this exercise side-on to a mirror so that you can check your alignment. Position yourself on all fours, with your hands directly under your shoulders, your knees directly under your hips, and your feet relaxed. Your spine should be in a neutral position, with the head in line with the spine and your eyes looking down at the floor. Breathe in.

2 Breathe out drawing your abdominals upward and inward toward the spine, curl the tailbone under the hips and arch the mid-back. The head should relax down toward the floor without overstretching the neck. The shoulders are pulling down in to the back to avoid hunching them. Inhale in this position. Breathe out to return to the neutral starting position. Initiate both movements from your the tailbone. Repeat five times.

3 Relax back into the rest position (illustrated).

This exercise increases the flexibility of the spine, moving and articulating it smoothly while maintaining a strong centre.

SPINE TWIST

1 Sit on a chair with your back straight and your feet hip-width apart. Your arms are folded in front of your chest, elbows lifted, shoulders down. Breathe in, lengthening up through the spine.

2 Breathe out, draw in your abdominals and lift the pelvic floor as you twist your spine to the right. The hips should remain stable and the weight evenly distributed on each buttock. The shoulder blades are sliding down. Breathe in to return to your starting position. Repeat on the left. VARIATION (not illustrated): You can also practise this exercise standing using a pole. Start with your feet hip-width apart and place a pole or broom handle (1.5–2m/5–6ft) across the back of the shoulders, about half-way down your shoulder blades, so your hands rest on the ends. Breathe in. Remember, strong abdominals and stable pelvis. Breathe out to twist the spine to the right. Imagine your head being pulled up toward the ceiling. Repeat seven times to alternate sides. This exercise complements the Hip Rolls in Chapter 3 (page 48).

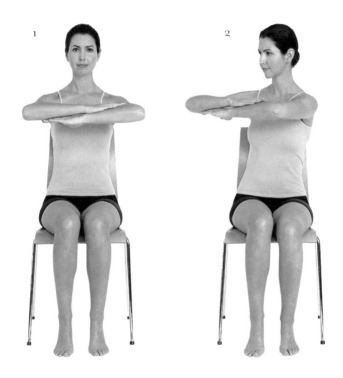

This exercise rotates the spine, working the waist while stabilizing the pelvis. If you use the pole it will also work the area
between the shoulder blades, and open the shoulders.

You *are* the truth
from foot to brow.
Now what else would
you like to know?

RUMI

(1207-1273)

Whoever is soft and yielding is a disciple of life.
The hard and stiff will be broken.
The soft and supple will prevail.

LAO TZU

(6TH CENTURY BCE)

KNEELING STAR

1 This is a challenging exercise for pelvic and shoulder stability as well as core stability. Start on all fours in the same alignment as the cat stretch (page 66): spine and pelvis in a neutral position, with the abdominals lifted. Breathe in. Breathe out and slide the right foot along the floor to stretch and lift the leg without moving the left hip. The leg should feel long and your back and abdominals strong. Breathe in. Breathe out to carefully replace the knee to the starting position. Repeat five more times, alternating legs.

2 Once you feel strong enough, you can include an arm stretch into the exercise. As you breathe out to extend and lift the leg, lengthen the opposite arm away from the shoulder without disturbing your shoulder stability. Imagine you have spirit levels across the back of the shoulders and the back of the hips to keep them level. Keep looking at the floor so that your neck does not bend. Feel energy reaching from your fingers of the extended arm and toes of the lifted leg.

Maintain your stability and strong centre in this exercise to ensure your back and buttock muscles work efficiently.

NECK ROLLS AND CIRCLES

1 Lie on your back with your legs outstretched and fully relaxed. If you have a lower-back problem, bend the knees into the relaxation position or rest your feet and lower legs up on a chair for support. Use a small cushion to support your head. Allow the head to sink heavily and the back of the neck to relax completely. Roll your head gently and slowly from side to side, just letting it roll naturally without forcing it. Be aware if one side feels more restricted. Repeat nine times.

2 Now gently nod the head slightly forward and slightly back still maintaining heaviness in the head and neck. Feel a gentle stretch at the back of the neck as you nod and the front of the neck as you take the head back.

3 Circle the head clockwise five times and anticlockwise five times. Start with a tiny circle getting slowly larger and then reverse it so that you start with the biggest circles gradually getting smaller. These exercises can be practised seated, but are most beneficial when the head is resting, being pulled by gravity.

All these exercises help to alleviate neck tension and increase mobility in the neck.

SHOULDER AND CHEST STRETCH

1 Stand with your feet hip-width apart. Hold on to a stretch band or scarf with your arms outstretched a bit wider than shoulder-width apart, level with your chest. Breathe in and lift up your arms above your head without raising your shoulders.

2 Breathe out, stretch the band and bend your elbows as you pull the band down behind your shoulders. Be careful not to arch your back, or poke your chin forward as this will strain the neck. Breathe in to lift your arms up over your head. If the pull across the shoulders feels uncomfortable, hold the band so that your hands are wider apart. Breathe out to bring your arms back down to starting position. Repeat four to seven times.

This exercise aims to increase mobility in the shoulder joints. It will stretch the muscles across the upper chest and the front of the shoulders and work the muscles of the upper back between the shoulder blades. It will also work the "lats" if you are pulling the shoulders down into the back.

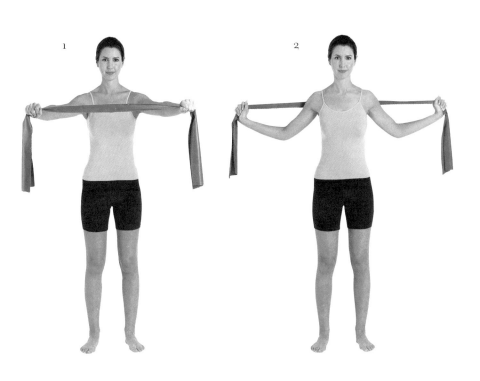

SHOULDER DROPS

1   This is a wonderful way to unwind the upper body if you have been working at a computer, driving, or generally straining the neck and shoulders. You may also benefit from practising shoulder drops in the morning if you sleep in an awkward position and you wake up feeling head, neck or shoulder tension. Lie in your relaxation position with the arms raised toward the ceiling, palms facing each other directly over the shoulders. Allow the backs of your shoulders to feel heavy. Use a small head cushion if needed. Breathe in as you reach up with one arm lifting the shoulder off the floor. Feel the fingers lengthen toward the ceiling to help you reach higher.

2   Breathe out to drop the shoulder back down to the floor. Breathe in to repeat with the other arm, lengthening it upward but keeping the elbow soft. Breathe out to drop the shoulder back down. You can practise this using one arm at a time, or both arms together. Additionally you can try pulling one arm diagonally across the body as you reach up for an extra shoulder stretch.

1

2

The aim of the exercise is to release tension in the upper body,
neck and shoulders.

ARM OPENINGS

1 Lie on your side with your head resting on a fairly plump cushion so that the head is in line with your neck and spine. The correct positioning of the body is essential for this exercise. Your knees are bent so that they are almost at a right angle to your hips and the feet are at a right angle to your knees. Your spine is straight, as if it is resting against a wall. Place a small cushion between your knees if you have hip problems. Stretch your arms out at shoulder height, palms together.

2 Breathe in to lift the top arm in an arc over the body turning the head gently to look at it. Breathe out to open the arm further out without lifting the shoulder. Keep your abdominals pulled in to protect the lower back. Breathe in to start bringing the arm back up and breathe out to rest the working arm back on to your other arm. Repeat five times on each side.

The aim is to stretch the muscles of the upper chest, shoulder and upper arm while keeping a strong centre.

1

2

the arms, legs and feet

Having focused on the trunk of the body in Chapter 4, we are now going to work on our limbs. In everyday life we often lift heavy loads, so it is important we learn how to use the right muscles to lift properly.

Initially it is a good idea to practise each exercise without weights, until you can do it correctly. Make sure you are able to practise the full recommended number of repetitions of the arm and leg exercises while maintaining stability in your shoulders and pelvis, and strength in your abdominal centre. Later you can introduce light weights.

The use of weights does not mean you will build up muscle bulk. As long as you use light weights and carry out the exercises correctly you will build up strength and your muscles will look more toned. Research has shown that weight-bearing exercises can also help to prevent or alleviate osteoporosis.

Our feet are our foundations – they bear our entire weight and are our point of contact with the earth. They are also probably the most neglected part of our body! If your feet are weak or poorly aligned, the knees, hips and pelvis will suffer, especially as you grow older. Many people think that walking exercises the feet. In fact walking exercises the legs, while the feet need specific exercises to really articulate the bones and work the muscles.

BICEP CURLS

1   You can practise this exercise standing or seated. You
will need light weights to start with – from 1 to 2 kilos
(2–4lb). If you don't have weights, use two small spice
jars. Stand with the feet hip-width apart holding the
weights with your palms facing in toward your hips.

2   Breathe in. Breathe out as you bend your right arm lifting the weight up to your shoulder. Your palm is facing
your shoulder, and your elbow remains close to your
body. Breathe in to return your arm to the starting position. Breathe out to repeat with the same arm. Keep your
shoulders pulled down into your back and stabilized
throughout the exercise. Your spine remains lengthened
and your abdominals strong. Be careful not to lean back
as you lift the arm. Keep the elbow isolated and still.
Repeat six to eight times with each arm. Once you are
familiar with the exercise, lift each arm alternately.

*The aim of this exercise is to strengthen the bicep muscles
while stabilizing the shoulder girdle.*

1

2

PEC FLY

1 Lie in the relaxation position with a small pillow under your head and one between your knees. Holding light weights extend your arms toward the ceiling so they are over the middle of your breastbone, palms facing each other. Bend your arms slightly so the elbows do not lock.

2 Breathe in as you open the arms outward toward the floor. You should be able to see the weights within your peripheral vision without resting the arms on the floor. Breathe out to return the arms to the starting position. Breathe in to open the arms again. Keep your spine and pelvis neutral. Imagine you are drawing an arc shape in the air as you open and close the arms and be careful not to grip the weights too tightly. Gently squeeze the cushion between the knees just enough to activate the inner thighs but without tilting the pelvis. Repeat six to eight times, fewer if you feel tension at the back of the neck.

The aim of this exercise is to tone the pectoral (chest) and upper-arm muscles, while stabilizing the shoulder girdle.

1

2

BACKSTROKE SWIMMING

1   This exercise is particularly beneficial for people with rounded shoulders. Lie in the relaxation position with a small cushion under your head and between your knees. Holding light weights, hold your arms up toward the ceiling so that your hands are a little forward of your shoulders. Your palms face away from your head and your elbows are slightly relaxed. Breathe in.

2   Breathe out as you take your left arm back toward the floor without the left shoulder lifting, and your right arm down toward the side of your right hip. Do not rest the arms on the floor. Breathe in to bring both arms back over the chest and repeat on the other side. The arm that is reaching back should never be too close to your ear. Keep it a little wider than your shoulder. Breathe in to bring the arms up again, really focusing on sliding your shoulders down in to your back so that your "lats" are helping you lift the arms away from gravity rather than straining the tops of the shoulders or the back of the neck. Repeat six to eight times on each side.

1

2

The aim of the exercise is to strengthen the muscles at the front of the shoulder and the "lats" while stabilizing the shoulder girdle. It will also help to open the shoulder blades.

TRICEPS LIFTS

1 Lie on the floor in the prone position with your forehead resting on a small cushion. Your arms are down by your sides with your palms facing your thighs. Breathe in.

2 Breathe out as you slide your shoulder blades down and lift the arms a little way off the ground. The elbows should be soft and the abdominals strong so that the spine does not arch. Breathe in to hold the position and breathe out to lower the arms with control.

VARIATION (not illustrated): You can also practise this exercise sitting in a chair. You need one without sides. Sit with your back straight, feet slightly parted and your shoulders down. Take a breath in. Breathe out to pull the arms behind your shoulder line without moving the shoulders. Breathe in to return the arms. When practising both exercises try holding the arms for a few seconds in the lifted position to further challenge the triceps.

This exercise strengthens and tones the triceps muscle at the back of the upper arm, an area prone to flabbiness.

1

2

LEG LIFTS AND CIRCLES

1   Begin by lying prone on the floor, arms bent, your hands under your forehead. Your legs are slightly parted, abdominals lifted and pelvis in neutral. Breathe in.

2   Breathe out as you lift your right leg away from the floor being careful not to lift the right hip. Breathe in to lower the leg, and breathe out to repeat with the left leg. Keep your shoulders as relaxed as you can and try to initiate the movement from a strong centre. The leg should not lift too high. Feel your pubic bone and hip bones connecting to the floor and the abdominals lifting. Repeat six to eight times.

VARIATION (not illustrated): Repeat the same exercise, lifting the leg and circling it five times one way and five times the other before lowering it back down. This will challenge your abdominals and buttock muscles a little more as well as your ability to stabilize the pelvis.

During both exercises, make sure that you keep the circles small, and keep your shoulders down and your upper body relaxed, lengthening through the legs.

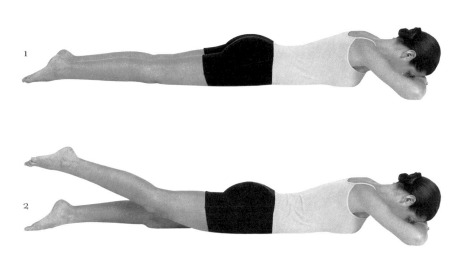

The aim of these exercises is to strengthen the buttocks and tone the backs of the legs without disturbing the position of the pelvis.

HIP FLEXOR STRETCH

1 The hip flexors comprise three muscles that are responsible for bending the knee toward the chest and bending the trunk forward from the waist. Tightness in this area can affect the alignment of the pelvis on the spine, causing the lower back to arch. Begin lying in the relaxation position, arms down at your sides. Breathe in.

2 Breathe out and lift your right knee toward your chest, allowing the thigh bone to drop into the hip joint. Breathe in to place both hands below the knee to pull the thigh toward your chest. Breathe out and slide the left leg along the floor, stretching and lengthening it without arching the back. Remain in this position for five breaths, as you inhale release your right leg a little. As you exhale pull it closer to your chest. Try to lengthen the back of your left thigh toward the floor without tilting the pelvis or arching the back. Keep the abdominals strong as you lift the left leg toward your chest to change to the other side.

The aim of the exercise is to stretch and work the hip flexors
while maintaining neutral pelvis and spine.

SINGLE LEG STRETCH

1 This is a good exercise to practise after the hip flexor stretch, as the hip joints will have released a little giving you more freedom of movement in the legs. Start in the relaxation position. Breathe in. Breathe out and pull the right knee gently toward your chest, so that your pelvis stays in neutral. Breathe in. Breathe out and slide the left leg along the floor. Feel it stretching and lengthening. Now pull in your abdominals, and lift the stretched leg off the floor. Keeping your neutral pelvis, inhale to bend the left knee towards the chest and exhale to stretch the right leg in the air. Repeat the exercise eight times, changing from one leg to the other without dropping the legs to the floor.

2 When you are strong enough, try the exercise with the upper body curled up. Be careful not to strain your neck in this position.

This exercise will strengthen and tone your legs and challenge your abdominal muscles.

1

2

HAMSTRING STRETCH

1 The hamstrings comprise three muscles at the back of each thigh. Tight hamstrings restrict your flexibility and disrupt the alignment of the lower back and hips. You will need a stretch band or a scarf. Start in the relaxation position. Bend your right knee toward your chest to place the band or scarf over the sole of the foot. Rest your elbows on the floor so that your shoulders remain relaxed. Breathe in.

2 Breathe out to extend the leg outward and upward until you feel a stretch at the back of the thigh. Be careful not to lock the knee. Remember your pelvis is in neutral so do not tuck under or lift the tailbone. Remain in this position for a few seconds breathing normally and then breathe in to bend the leg half-way toward the chest. Repeat five to seven times on each leg. If you want to increase the stretch in to the lower leg, try flexing the ankle so that the foot is pulling toward your face. You will feel the back of the calf stretching. Always keep the spine and pelvis in neutral.

This exercise is a workout for all the muscles at the back of the leg, particularly if you incorporate a foot flex (see page 108).

OUTER THIGH LIFT

1 Lie on your right side with both knees bent, your feet at a right angle to your knees. Extend your right arm under your ear and place a small cushion between your ear and shoulder. Your left shoulder should be over your right and your left hip over your right. Your left hand rests on the floor in front of your chest. Feel lifted on the right side of your waist rather than sinking into the floor.

2 Draw in your abdominals. Breathe in to extend the left leg to hip height and flex the foot forward.

3 Breathe out to lift the leg about 10cm (4in) above hip height. Breathe in to lower just to hip height. Repeat seven times with each leg. As you lift and lower engage your abdominal muscles to keep the hip stable. If you rotate the leg slightly inward from the hip it will work the outer thigh muscle more. Relax your head and neck, and keep the shoulders down into your back.

The aim of this exercise is to strengthen the buttock and outer-thigh muscles while maintaining pelvic and lumbar stability.

1

2

3

THE OYSTER

1 Lie on your right side as in the previous exercise but this time place your feet further back toward your buttocks. Keep your right arm lengthened away from the right shoulder and relax your head heavily into the cushion. Draw your abdominals in and feel lifted on the right side of your waist. Your left hip is directly over the right and the left knee and foot directly over the right. Breathe in.

2 Breathe out to lift the left knee away from the right while keeping the feet together. You are rotating the thigh from within your left hip while keeping the pelvis completely still. Imagine an oyster shell opening. Breathe in to lower the thigh with control. Repeat five to seven times on each side. With every repetition try to open your knee a little higher. You may find it useful to place your hand on your hip to keep it stabilized. Maintain your strong centre throughout this exercise.

The aim of this exercise is to strengthen the buttock muscles and stabilize the torso and pelvis.

1

2

INNER THIGH LIFT

1   Lie on your right side with your left knee resting on a cushion. Ideally it wants to be at the same height as your hip so that your pelvis does not roll forward. The spine should be lengthened and your right arm extended away from your shoulder. Rest your head on a small cushion placed between the ear and shoulder. Your right leg is stretched and slightly in front of the hip. Breathe in.

2   Breathe out and lift your right leg, feeling the top of the inner thigh working. Stretch the leg away, and for extra effect rotate it to the right. Point or flex your foot. Breathe in to lower the leg with control, without fully relaxing it on the floor. Repeat seven to nine times with each leg. To challenge the inner thighs more, hold the leg up for longer before lowering it back down. The difficulty in this exercise is keeping the rest of the body correctly positioned so you move only the working leg.

The aim of this exercise is to strengthen the muscles of your inner thigh. It will also work your buttock muscles.

1

2

INNER THIGH SQUEEZE

1 Lie in the relaxation position with your feet together. Place a large folded pillow or plump cushion between your knees. Relax your arms by your sides. Breathe in. Breathe out as you squeeze the knees and inner thighs together, maintaining neutral pelvis and neutral spine. Keep the abdominals pulling in, the pelvic floor lifting and the shoulders relaxed. Breathe in to release. Repeat nine times holding the squeeze a little longer each time.

2 You can practise this exercise on either your back or your front. To do the exercise lying on your front simply place a smaller cushion between the tops of the thighs and lie with your forehead resting on your folded hands. Relax the neck and shoulders. Your toes are together and heels apart. Begin with your legs relaxed. Breathe in. Breathe out as you draw the inner thighs together, and turn your legs out from the hips. Gently squeeze the cushion, keeping the abdominals lifted. Inhale to release the legs and buttocks. Repeat nine more times.

1

2

This exercise strengthens the inner thighs. Additionally it will work the abdominals, buttocks and pelvic floor.

FOOT EXERCISES

Point and flex You can practise this exercise sitting with your legs outstretched or you can incorporate it into your Hamstring stretch (see page 98), using the stretch band around the foot for extra resistance.

1 "Point" the foot softly away from your body while keeping the foot in the correct alignment with your knee and hip. Be careful not to twist the ankle inward so that the foot looks "sickled" or banana-shaped.

2 "Flex" by bending the ankle so that the toes and ball of the foot pull toward the body. Point and flex ten times.

Circling (not illustrated): Again you can carry out this exercise seated or with the band round the foot.

1 Point the toes away from your body. Pull the toes inward toward each other, then flex the ankles toward you and finally twist the feet outward away from each other. This completes a full circle.

2 Repeat this way nine more times and then circle the feet in the opposite direction ten times.

These exercises strengthen and mobilize the ankles and metatarsals, and work the flexors and extensors of the foot.

pilates living

Now you have learned some basic Pilates exercises you can decide how to fit them into your everyday schedule. Try practising early in the morning before you go to work or take the kids to school, or perhaps at lunchtime or early in the evening. In this chapter I have outlined some ten-minute workouts. On average a Pilates class will last 1 hour to 1 hour 15 minutes.

Pilates can benefit you greatly if you are pregnant. During pregnancy you will undergo many emotional, physical and hormonal changes. The slow controlled movements of Pilates exercises are very safe during pregnancy as they will not stress your joints. With its emphasis on posture, which can change a lot during pregnancy, it will prepare you for labour, help make your pregnancy more comfortable and help you regain your figure after the birth. Check with your doctor before embarking on any of the exercises and practise only if your doctor is happy for you to do so.

Pilates is also extremely effective when combined with other sports. In this section I have mentioned a few common sports that can be greatly enhanced with the introduction of some Pilates exercises.

The section on relaxation is an ideal way to close your exercise session as it provides active relaxation for the whole body and mind, without losing the sense of energy that you have created during your workout.

PILATES SEQUENCES

Mix and match these workouts according to which area you feel needs work. Gradually you can build up so that your session consists of a five-minute warm-up, 40–50 minutes of exercises and a ten-minute relaxation.

Ten-minute Sequence: Standing / Seated
Spine twist (pages 68–69)
Neck rolls & circles (pages 74–75)
Shoulder & chest stretch (pages 76–77)
Foot rises (p. 38) / exercises (pages 108–109) if seated

Ten-minute Back Sequence
Side hip rolls (pages 48–49)
Spine curls (pages 60–61)
Cat stretch and rest position (pages 66–67)
Spine roll-down (p. 37)

Ten-minute Neck & Shoulder Sequence
Shoulder & chest stretch (pages 76–77)

Shoulder drops (pages 78–79)
Arm openings (pages 80–81)
Neck rolls and circles (pages 74–75)

Ten-minute Leg Sequence

Hip flexor & single leg stretch (pages 96–97)
Hamstring stretch (pages 98–99)
Inner thigh squeeze (pages 106–107)
Outer thigh lift (pages 100–101)

Ten-minute Abdominal Sequence

Abdominal curl-ups (pages 44–45)
Oblique curl-ups (pages 46–47)
The hundred (pages 50–51)
Curl-downs (pages 52–53)

Ten-minute Arm Sequence

Bicep curls (pages 84–85)
Pec fly (pages 86–87)
Backstroke swimming (pages 88–89)
Triceps lifts (pages 90–91)

PILATES FOR SPORTS

The muscles we use during sports require strengthening and stretching to work properly. Pilates is the ideal exercise method for sports people as it establishes a strong postural base from which they can safely develop sporting techniques. In addition many common sports are unilateral, meaning that they develop one side of the body or one set of muscles more than the others.

It is a good idea to stretch the body at the beginning of a sports session and again at the end. Stretching at the beginning will warm up and loosen stiff muscles, while stretching at the end cools down the body, relaxing tired muscles. Here are a few recommended exercises for some common sports:

Golf
This is a sport that uses one side of the body more than the other. Areas prone to injury from the swinging action or lifting heavy clubs are the lower spine, the hips, the neck, the shoulders and the forearms.

Pec fly · Arm openings · Spine roll-down · Spine twist · Shoulder and chest stretch · Side hip rolls · Neck rolls and circles · Abdominal curl-ups · Oblique curl-ups.

Soccer

Soccer players tend to have strong but tight hamstrings, overworked quadriceps (the muscle on the front of the thighs) and tight hip-flexor muscles caused by the repetitive kicking action. Their buttock muscles, calf muscles and ankles are also usually tight.

Spine roll-down · Spine curls · Hip flexor stretch · Hamstring stretch · Abdominal curl-ups · Foot point and flex · Circling · Leg lifts and circles

Running

Jogging and running put particular strain on the ankles especially if your trainers aren't designed for running. The leg muscles are usually strong and need to be stretched out before and after exercise.

Hamstring stretch · Hip flexor stretch · Foot point and flex · Ankle circles · Shoulder and chest stretch

Racket sports

Tennis, squash and badminton involve repetitive movements with the arm and shoulder as well as some rotation of the trunk. Most of us are predominantly left- or right-handed, so racket sports tend to use one side of the body more than the other. Pilates exercises can help prevent injury by rebalancing the body.

Neck rolls and circles · Shoulder drops · Arm openings · Spine curls · Spine twist · Shoulder and chest stretch · Foot point and flex · Circling · Spine roll-down · Cat stretch and rest position

Swimming

Depending on which stroke you practise, swimmers are susceptible to various weaknesses. For example if you practise breast stroke with your head out of the water, your neck and lower back will be strained. Backstroke tends slightly to impinge the shoulder joints.

The dart · Shoulder drops · Backstroke swimming · Arm openings · Abdominal curl-ups · Spine extension · Cat stretch and rest position · Hip flexor stretch

RELAXATION

Relaxing at the end of your exercise session will give both your mind and body a chance to absorb the benefits of your practice. Alternatively you might like to practise some relaxation and breathing simply to unwind at the end of a busy day or a long journey. Both these relaxation and breathing exercises are best practised in a quiet, warm room with some gentle relaxation music in the background. Allow 10 to 15 minutes for each exercise.

Breathing to relax

1 Lie either in the relaxation position or supporting your legs on a chair or bed. Place a small pillow under your head and your hands on your lower ribcage so that your middle fingers touch. You may find it useful to place a book on your abdomen so that you can feel the way that it moves up and down as you breathe.

2 Breathe in deeply from your diaphragm. Focus your attention on your abdomen, which should rise as you inhale. This is different from the lateral thoracic

breathing outlined in Chapter 1, which is used during Pilates exercises. Now we are focusing on the ribcage expanding and the abdominals rising on the inhalation.

3 Breathe out slowly through your mouth and feel how your ribs are closing and your abdomen is lowering. Remember that inhalation should re-energize or "inspire" as you are taking in more oxygen. In contrast the exhalation encourages relaxation or "expiration". If you practise this breathing in your everyday life, even while at work or when travelling, you will be amazed at how it can help de-stress and re-energize you.

Progressive muscular relaxation

1 This form of relaxation relieves tension by relaxing muscle groups individually. The idea is to work progressively through the body, systematically flexing and relaxing different muscle groups. Lie on your back with your legs hip-width apart and completely relaxed, arms stretched back behind your head with the backs of the hands resting on the floor. Close your eyes and allow the whole body to feel heavy.

2   Stretch your fingers and toes as if you are being stretched by your extremities. Feel the tension in the muscles of your hands and feet and hold for a count of ten before completely relaxing. Now stretch your calves, knees and elbows while keeping your fingers and toes relaxed. You are aiming to isolate one area of the body from another. Hold for a count of ten and then relax.

3   Repeat, this time tightening your buttocks and thighs. Then move on to your abdominal area, pulling in the abdominal muscles and lifting the pelvic floor. Hold for ten counts, then relax. Move up to the shoulders – for this part you may prefer to have your arms by your sides. Slide the shoulders right up to your ears so that your neck disappears. Relax and slide them down in to your back so that your neck becomes long again.

4   Remain still for a while feeling all the tension melt away from your body. Breathe slowly and deeply, and feel your body sinking into the floor. When you are ready, become aware of the sounds around you and the floor beneath you again. Gently roll on to your side and stay there for a few moments before opening your eyes and sitting up.

FINDING A TEACHER

If you decide you would like to attend a class instead of or in addition to practising at home, make sure you check the teacher's credentials first. Look for a teacher with Body Control Pilates Association, Pilates Foundation or Pilates Institute after their name. On the internet under these headings you should be able to find listings of the teachers in or near your area.

Pilates is a precise form of exercise and if it is not taught and performed correctly it could do more harm than good. Don't be afraid to ask a teacher where they trained – after all, it's your body in their hands so it is important to have peace of mind. Ideally never attend a class that has more than 12 people in it. Note that many physiotherapists are also qualified Pilates teachers. It is also a good idea to check the credentials of your teacher with the Exercise Register (www.exerciseregister.org).

If you have difficulty finding an exercise mat or a stretch band, there are a number of excellent suppliers whose details can be found on the internet.

QUICK PILATES CHECKLIST

Just to re-cap here are a few important facts:

- **Do** practise in a warm, quiet room.
- **Do** wear comfortable, practical clothes.
- **Do** concentrate on the precision and control of each exercise, especially maintaining your strong centre.
- **Do** always check that your whole body is correctly aligned and relaxed before and during exercise.
- **Do** keep the focus on your breathing. It should be deep, slow and rhythmical. Breathe in through your nose and out through your mouth.
- **Do** keep your awareness of your body as a whole, not just the area you are moving.
- **Do** practise the breathing and relaxation exercises on pages 118–120 at the end of your exercise session.
- **Do** consult your doctor before starting any exercise regime, particularly if you are pregnant.
- **Don't** rush any of the exercises.
- **Don't** try to practise too many repetitions, or to introduce weights, until you're used to the exercises.

I have learned this at least by my experiment: that if one advances confidently in the direction of his dreams, and endeavors to live the life which he has imagined, he will meet with a success unexpected in common hours.

HENRY DAVID THOREAU

(1817–1862)

INDEX

PICTURE CREDITS / ACKNOWLEDGMENTS

Picture Credits

The publisher would like to thank the following people and photographic libraries for permission to reproduce their material. Every care has been taken to trace copyright holders. However, if we have omitted anyone we apologize and will, if informed, make corrections in any future edition.

Page 2 Getty/Taxi/Clarissa Leahy; **17** Getty/Image Bank/Jasper James; **30** Getty/Stone/Ryan/Beyer; **41** Getty/Stone/Dave Schiefelbein; **56** Rubberball Productions; **71** Getty/Photographer's Choice/Marc Schlossman; **116** Getty/Taxi/ John Cocking; **121** ZEFA/O Graf; **122** Getty/Taxi/Clarissa Leahy

Author's Acknowledgments

I would like to thank Matthew Ward for his brilliant photography and Caroline Long, the model, for her patience and beauty. Also all those at Duncan Baird for their contribution toward the production of this book: Grace Cheetham and Zoë Fargher (Editors) and Justin Ford (Designer).

Publisher's Acknowledgments

Model: Caroline Long
Make-up artist: Tinks Reding